NO
FAILING
STUDENTS

SEVEN TEACHING STRATEGIES I USED AS A
TEACHER TO TAKE SMART BUT PROBLEMATIC
STUDENTS FROM FAILURE TO SUCCESS IN ONE
ACADEMIC QUARTER (45 DAYS)

DIANE HUNT

No Failing Students

Diane Hunt

Copyright© 2015

ISBN-13: 978-1505684469

Cover Design by Sean O'Connor
OhSeeDesign.com

Printed in the United States of America

TABLE OF CONTENTS

No Failing Students

No Failing Students is a method of teaching that uses higher-order thinking skills where failure is not an option. It works in elementary and middle school, and through high school, in all subject areas.

It is important to note that we will do this not by watering down the curriculum, but by using higher-order thinking skills like analyzing, evaluating, and creating.

STEP 1:

CORE VOCABULARY

STEP 1:

Core Vocabulary

The first step is to find about 30 words representing the core vocabulary words for the course you are teaching. These words will differ based on your grade level and subject area.

After you have determined these 30 essential words, develop a pre-test. You can place the words at the top and the definitions at the bottom. When you get your results, make a list of the students who scored below 90% on this pre-assessment of vocabulary words.

This step accomplishes two major purposes:

➤ It helps you identify the vocabulary that is essential for learning in your classroom.

➤ It also allows you to identify which students are struggling to comprehend these vocabulary words and the content that surrounds them.

Date _____ Name _____

ELEMENTARY VOCABULARY
PRE-ASSESSMENT EXAMPLE
(Include no more than 15 words)

Directions: Fill in the blanks below with the correct word from the top of the page.

Amaze	Analyze	Arranged
Connection	Cooperation	Cycle
Diagram	Different	Drowsy
Effect	Enormous	Estimate

1._____
   calculate roughly or rough calculation

2._____
   huge, gigantic, giant

3._____
   result or accomplish

4._____
   sleepy, dozy

5._____
   unlike or separate

6._____
   drawing, sketch

7._____
   round or a bike, pedal

8._____

teamwork

9._____

link, relationship

10._____

order, organize

11._____

examine, inspect

12._____

surprise, shock

Date _____ Name _____

MIDDLE SCHOOL VOCABULARY
PRE-ASSESSMENT EXAMPLE
(Include no more than 30 words at a time)

Directions: Fill in the blanks below with the correct word from the top of the page.

Abdicate	Abrasive	Abruptly
Belligerent	Bewilder	Bias
Candor	Casualty	Cause
Dawdle	Deceitful	Demeanor

1. _____
   source, root, or principle, ideal

2. _____
   baffle, mystify, puzzle, confuse

3. _____
   resign, retire, step down

4. _____
   hostile, aggressive, threatening

5. _____
   victim, fatality, loss, MIA

6. _____
   manner, air, attitude, appearance, look

7._____
   frankness, openness, honesty

8._____
   dishonest, untruthful, false

9._____
   corrosive, cutting, biting

10._____
   suddenly, unexpectedly, curtly, bluntly

11._____
   prejudice, partiality, favoritism

12._____
   linger, dally, idle

Date _____ Name _____

HIGH SCHOOL VOCABULARY
PRE-ASSESSMENT EXAMPLE

(Include no more than 30 words at a time)

Directions: Fill in the blanks below with the correct word from the top of the page.

Aberration	Abstract	Accolade
Cajole	Callous	Capitulate
Dearth	Decadence	Deference
Effervescent	Egregious	Equivocal

1. _____

   conceptual, intellectual, extract, separate

2. _____

   anomaly, deviation, divergence, abnormality

3. _____

   honor, privilege, award, gift, title

4. _____

   surrender, yield, submit

5. _____

   heartless, unfeeling, uncaring, cold

6. _____

   persuade, coax, seduce

7. _____

   dissipation, corruption, sin, immorality

8._____

respect, respectfulness, dutifulness

9._____

lack, scarcity, shortage, shortfall, want,
deficiency

10._____

fizzy, sparkling, carbonated, gassy, bubbly

11._____

ambiquous, indefinite, noncommittal, vague

12._____

shocking, appalling, terrible, awful

Free No Failing
Students Resources...

I have prepared a set of tools that can help you pre-assess your students. All of the following resources are free and downloadable...

- Elementary School Pre-assessment Template

- Middle School Pre-assessment Template

- High School Pre-assessment Template

To download your Free Productivity package (which includes these pre-assessment templates), go to:

http://www.NoFailingStudents.com

Either click the link if you are using a digital book reader or type it into your browser.

STEP 2:

IDENTIFYING MULTIPLE INTELLIGENCES

STEP 2:

Identifying Multiple Intelligences

Step two of our seven-step process is finding out which intelligence the students find easiest to learn in. So we want to survey the students' preferred multiple intelligence.

I like to use multiple intelligences, rather than learning styles, because it's divided into smaller groups, which makes it easier for me to zero in on the intelligence that the student finds easiest to learn in.

For those educators not familiar with Multiple Intelligence, there are at least eight different categories of learners. These intelligences help teachers identify the best way for students to learn and understand new material.

The intelligences include:

> Naturalist
> Mathematical logical
> Verbal linguistic
> Musical rhythmic
> Visual spatial
> Bodily kinesthetic
> Interpersonal
> Intrapersonal

It is important for the teacher to identify the students who did poorly on the vocabulary assessment from Step One and see which multiple intelligences they favor.

MULTIPLE INTELLIGENCES SURVEY

© 1999 Walter McKenzie,
The One and Only Surfaquarium
http://surfaquarium.com/MI/inventory.htm

Part I

Complete each section by placing a "1" next to each statement you feel accurately describes you. If you do not identify with a statement, leave the space provided blank. Then total the column in each section.

SECTION 1

_____ I enjoy categorizing things by common traits

_____ Ecological issues are important to me

_____ Classification helps me make sense of new data

_____ I enjoy working in a garden

_____ I believe preserving our National Parks is important

_____ Putting things in hierarchies makes sense to me

_____ Animals are important in my life

_____ My home has a recycling system in place

_____ I enjoy studying biology, botany and/or zoology

_____ I pick up on subtle differences in meaning

_____ TOTAL for Section 1

SECTION 2

_____ I easily pick up on patterns

_____ I focus in on noise and sounds

_____ Moving to a beat is easy for me

_____ I enjoy making music

_____ I respond to the cadence of poetry

_____ I remember things by putting them in a rhyme

_____ Concentration is difficult for me if there is background noise

_____ Listening to sounds in nature can be very relaxing

_____ Musicals are more engaging to me than dramatic plays

_____ Remembering song lyrics is easy for me

_____ TOTAL for Section 2

SECTION 3

_____ I am known for being neat and orderly

_____ Step-by-step directions are a big help

_____ Problem solving comes easily to me

_____ I get easily frustrated with disorganized people

_____ I can complete calculations quickly in my head

_____ Logic puzzles are fun

_____ I can't begin an assignment until I have all my "ducks in a row"

_____ Structure is a good thing

_____ I enjoy troubleshooting something that isn't working properly

_____ Things have to make sense to me or I am dissatisfied

_____ TOTAL for Section 3

SECTION 4

_____ It is important to see my role in the "big picture" of things

_____ I enjoy discussing questions about life

_____ Religion is important to me

_____ I enjoy viewing art work

_____ Relaxation and meditation exercises are rewarding to me

_____ I like traveling to visit inspiring places

_____ I enjoy reading philosophers

_____ Learning new things is easier when I see their real-world application

_____ I wonder if there are other forms of intelligent life in the universe

_____ It is important for me to feel connected to people, ideas, and beliefs

_____ TOTAL for Section 4

SECTION 5

_____ I learn best interacting with others

_____ I enjoy informal chat and serious discussion

_____ The more, the merrier

_____ I often serve as a leader among peers and colleagues

_____ I value relationships more than ideas or accomplishments

_____ Study groups are very productive for me

_____ I am a "team player"

_____ Friends are important to me

_____ I belong to more than three clubs or organizations

_____ I dislike working alone

_____ TOTAL for Section 5

SECTION 6

_____ I learn by doing
_____ I enjoy making things with my hands
_____ Sports are a part of my life
_____ I use gestures and non-verbal cues when I communicate
_____ Demonstrating is better than explaining
_____ I love to dance
_____ I like working with tools
_____ Inactivity can make me more tired than being very busy
_____ Hands-on activities are fun
_____ I live an active lifestyle

_____ TOTAL for Section 6

SECTION 7

_____ Foreign languages interest me
_____ I enjoy reading books, magazines and web sites
_____ I keep a journal
_____ Word puzzles like crosswords or jumbles are enjoyable
_____ Taking notes helps me remember and understand
_____ I faithfully contact friends through letters and/or e-mail
_____ It is easy for me to explain my ideas to others
_____ I write for pleasure
_____ Puns, anagrams and spoonerisms are fun
_____ I enjoy public speaking and participating in debates

_____ TOTAL for Section 7

SECTION 8

_____ My attitude affects how I learn
_____ I like to be involved in causes that help others
_____ I am keenly aware of my moral beliefs
_____ I learn best when I have an emotional attachment to the subject
_____ Fairness is important to me
_____ Social justice issues interest me
_____ Working alone can be just as productive as working in a group
_____ I need to know why I should do something before I agree to do it
_____ When I believe in something, I give more effort toward it
_____ I am willing to protest or sign a petition to right a wrong

_____ TOTAL for Section 8

SECTION 9

_____ I can visualize ideas in my mind
_____ Rearranging a room and redecorating are fun for me
_____ I enjoy creating my own works of art
_____ I remember better using graphic organizers
_____ I enjoy all kinds of entertainment media
_____ Charts, graphs, and tables help me interpret data
_____ A music video can make me more interested in a song
_____ I can recall things as mental pictures
_____ I am good at reading maps and blueprints
_____ Three-dimensional puzzles are fun

_____ TOTAL for Section 9

Part II

Now carry forward your total from each section and multiply by 10 below:

Section	Total Forward	Multiply	Score
1		X10	
2		X10	
3		X10	
4		X10	
5		X10	
6		X10	
7		X10	
8		X10	
9		X10	

Part III

Now plot your scores on the bar graph provided:

	Sec 1	Sec 2	Sec 3	Sec 4	Sec 5	Sec 6	Sec 7	Sec 8	Sec 9
100									
90									
80									
70									
60									
50									
40									
30									
20									
10									
0									

Part IV

Now determine your intelligence profile!

Key:

Section 1 – This reflects your Naturalist strength

Section 2 – This suggests your Musical strength

Section 3 – This indicates your Logical strength

Section 4 – This illustrates your Existential strength

Section 5 – This shows your Interpersonal strength

Section 6 – This tells your Kinesthetic strength

Section 7 – This indicates your Verbal strength

Section 8 – This reflects your Intrapersonal strength

Section 9 – This suggests your Visual strength

Free No Failing Students Resources...

I have gathered multiple intelligence surveys that can help you motivate your students. All of the following resources are free and downloadable...

- Elementary school multiple intelligence surveys

- Middle school multiple intelligence surveys

- High school multiple intelligence surveys

To download your Free Productivity package (which includes these multiple intelligence surveys), go to:

http://www.NoFailingStudents.com

Either click the link if you are using a digital book reader or type it into your browser.

STEP 3:

RE-DESIGN PRACTICE

STEP 3:

Re-Design Practice

Step Three is one of the most important steps in the seven-step program. In Step Three, we re-design practice work, combining the student's preferred multiple intelligence with Bloom's Taxonomy of Higher Order Thinking Skills.

Blooms Taxonomy of Higher Order Thinking Skills includes different levels of skills and questions:

➢ **Remembering**: Recalling information. Recognizing, listing, describing, retrieving, naming, finding

➢ **Understanding**: Explaining ideas or concepts. Interpreting, summarizing, paraphrasing, classifying, explaining

➢ **Applying**: Using information in another familiar situation. Implementing, carrying out, using, executing

➢ **Analyzing**: Breaking information into parts to explore understandings and relationships. Comparing, organizing, deconstructing, interrogating, finding

> **Evaluating**: Justifying a decision or course of action. Checking, hypothesizing, critiquing, experimenting, judging

> **Creating**: Generating new ideas, products, or ways of viewing things. Designing, constructing, planning, producing, inventing

We want to concentrate on analyzing, evaluating, and creating. For people who believe you're watering down the curriculum or just making this easier, nothing could be further from the truth. You're just actually focusing on the top half of Bloom's Taxonomy. These are the three highest levels of Bloom's Taxonomy: analyzing; evaluating and creating. In this particular step, we're going to focus on creating practice assignments that analyze, evaluate, and create with different multiple intelligences.

In a particular assignment for a student, who scored below 90% on the pre-assessment, we will begin with analyzing. When we give tasks for analyzing, we don't always use the word "analyzing." There are similar terms, like classifying, outlining, diagramming, comparing, and contrasting. Also, when we're working with younger students, such as those in kindergarten, we might not use the term "analyze," but they most certainly can compare two items.

So even though our exercises or instructions don't use the words analyze or analyzing, if we're using words like classify, outline, diagram, compare, and contrast, we're still within that Bloom's category, and we are still using high-order thinking skills.

For example, a student who is a Naturalist in Multiple Intelligences might classify insects while working in the plant area. We have them at the level of analyzing and in an area that they feel comfortable in—the plant area.

A student in a kindergarten classroom who is mathematical might be comparing five items from the kitchen area.

For a middle school or high school linguistic student, we might be writing two paragraphs contrasting poets from the 19th century.

For a musical student, we might have them outline a chapter on banking while listening to music. Maybe this would be distracting to some students, so you might have students use earbuds, so those who like to listen to music wouldn't disturb the ones who do not like to listen to music.

If you are a visual learner, we might have you show comparisons using a Venn diagram.

An interpersonal learner could classify rocks with a partner, while an intrapersonal learner might compare two features from their project individually.

An elementary level example for a kinesthetic learner might be to stand at the back counter while separating fruit and vegetable pictures.

The verbs for each activity are outline, diagram, classify, but we are changing the activity each time to fit the multiple intelligence.

You might be thinking, "So I'm supposed to have 25 different assignments for 25 different students?" Or in my examples here, "So every day I have to come up with eight different assignments? Is that how this works?"

No, not really. Students like choices. I would come up with two choices from which the students can select. In addition, I would offer choices in areas where my students would be having the most difficulty. For example, if Student A is having a lot of difficulty, I would look into which multiple intelligence they prefer and offer a multiple intelligence activity that would fit their learning style.

You don't have to do all eight every day. My recommendation is to focus on some of the students who are struggling in class, pick their multiple intelligences, and focus on those two or three.

For the students who scored less than 90%, we focus on analyzing from Bloom's Taxonomy. For the students that scored 90% and above on the pre-assessment, they need practice using the highest-order thinking skills of evaluating and creating.

You don't have to recreate the wheel here. You already have one assignment. You can change it slightly to meet a different multiple intelligence, or you can have some students evaluate other students' work or even create new assignments for you as part of the higher parts of Bloom's Taxonomy. We want to concentrate on having students analyzing, evaluating, and creating, and not falling down into the lower levels of Bloom's Taxonomy of just remembering, understanding, and applying.

What I love about this is that a lot of teachers with struggling students (and it's a temptation that I've fallen into as well) fall into a drill-and-kill pattern where we give them busy work or memorization. We just give them comprehension questions. The greatest benefit is that you're really focusing on the higher-order thinking skills so these students have the same likelihood of success as the other students without being turned off or becoming bored. Instead, they're motivated.

ELEMENTARY EXAMPLES

Elementary examples	Bloom's Taxonomy		
Multiple Intelligences	Analyze	Evaluate	Create
Naturalist	Compare and contrast the most important points presented by two texts on the same topic while sitting in the plant area	Verify which line graphs are correct while sitting by the class pet	Write addition and subtraction sentences while sitting by the window
Mathematical - logical	Compare numbers up to 100	Detect which even or odd number comes before or after	Create word problems involving dollar bills, quarters, dimes, nickels and pennies
Verbal - linguistic	Compare adjectives and adverbs	Check subtraction word problems for correctness	Write subtraction sentences to describe pictures
Musical	Compare and contrast two versions of the same story while listening to music	Evaluate locomotor movements conducted to even and uneven beats	Create a song about capitalizing days, months and holidays

Spatial - visual	Compare metric units of volume using illustrations	Verify which bar graphs are correct	Create pictographs
Bodily-kinesthetic	Compare fractions using models	Moving from station to station decide if the sentences are past, present or future	Create a routine that includes two types of body rolls
Interpersonal	With a partner analyze sides and angles	Check a partner's math work by giving feedback on each problem	Create an audio recording of a story with a partner
Intrapersonal	Individually compare and contrast the function of the heart during rest and during physical activity	Individually judge whether the sources are primary or secondary	Write multiple sentences in an order that supports a story individually

MIDDLE SCHOOL EXAMPLES

Middle School examples	Bloom's Taxonomy		
Multiple Intelligences	Analyze	Evaluate	Create
Naturalist	Analyze cause and effect relationships between individuals and historical events while sitting in the plant area	Evaluate the argument and claims in a text, assessing whether the reasoning is sound and the evidence is relevant and sufficient to support claims while sitting by huge animal posters	Draw, construct, and describe geometrical figures and the relationships between them while sitting by the window
Mathematical - logical	Compare ratios in word problems	Evaluate variable expressions for numerators and denominators	Design and use a simulation to generate frequencies for compound events
Verbal linguistic	Choose between personal and reflexive pronouns	Critique the United States expanding role in the world during the late 19th and 20th centuries	Write an argument to support a claim with clear reasons and relevant evidence

Musical	Compare and order decimals while listening to music	Assess the credibility and accuracy of multiple print and digital sources while listening to music	Create a rap about proper warm up and cool down techniques for a physical activity
Spatial - Visual	Analyze the relationship between dependent and independent variables using graphs and tables.	Evaluate physical activity into moderate or vigorous using a Venn Diagram	Create a model of the interactions of living organisms within an ecosystem
Bodily-kinesthetic	Compare and contrast a variety of art forms with their own culture through performance	Evaluate fellow classmates work with a rubric while moving from seat to seat	Construct a model showing the positions of the earth, sun and moon as they relate to eclipses at the back counter
Interpersonal	Classify rocks and minerals by observable properties with a partner	Evaluate with a classmate, their argument and claims	Produce sherbet with a partner while learning about acids and bases
Intrapersonal	Analyze how two texts address a similar topic individually	Evaluate single-variable expressions individually	Construct and interpret scatter plots individually

HIGH SCHOOL EXAMPLES

High School examples	Bloom's Taxonomy		
Multiple Intelligences	**Analyze**	**Evaluate**	**Create**
Naturalist	Classify sequences while sitting by the window	Evaluate exponential functions while sitting in the atrium	Construct an equilateral triangle, a square and a regular hexagon inscribed in a circle while sitting by large animal posters
Mathematical - logical	Compare strategies on the basis of expected values	Evaluate reports based on data	Build a function that models a relationship between two quantities
Verbal - linguistic	Analyze an author's argument for making points clear, convincing and engaging	Evaluate a speaker's point of view, reasoning, and use of evidence	Write the probability distribution for a game of chance
Musical	Compare the Laws of Sines and Cosines while listening to music	Evaluate polynomials using synthetic division while listening to music	Create a rap on a technical process

Spatial - visual	Compare linear, quadratic, and exponential models	Evaluate information presented in diverse media and formats.	Create bar graphs, line graphs and histograms
Bodily-kinesthetic	Analyze a sequence of events by first charting the events on a large poster	Evaluate outcomes of decisions by role playing	Model polynomials with algebra tiles
Interpersonal	With a partner analyze the author's purpose in a text	With a partner evaluate multiple source of information presented in different formats to solve a problem	With a partner make geometric constructions
Intrapersonal	Individually analyze how the text structures ideas into categories	Individually evaluate the hypotheses, data, analysis and conclusion in a text	Individually write informative text on a scientific experiment

Free No Failing Students Resources...

I have gathered analyzing activities for you to use with your students to increase their higher order thinking skills. All of the following resources are free and downloadable...

- Elementary school analyzing activities

- Middle school analyzing activities

- High school analyzing activities

To download your Free Productivity package (which includes these analyzing activities), go to:

http://www.NoFailingStudents.com

Either click the link if you are using a digital book reader or type it into your browser.

STEP 4:

OFFER A CHOICE

STEP 4:

Offer a Choice

Step four in the seven-step process is offering students a choice of activities per lesson.

Students love choices. We know this, and we already have overlaid Bloom's Taxonomy against the multiple intelligences.

For example, let's say today I would like my students to analyze a graph. The choice might be to either analyze a graph individually, which is intrapersonal, or analyze a graph with a partner, which is interpersonal.

You don't need a different assignment for every student in your classroom, which is the fear teachers sometimes have. Here you just have two different assignments. As a matter of fact, it's really the same practice assignment; you're just giving them a choice in how to do it. Students like it because they have a choice.

The whole class will not choose to do it individually, nor will the whole class choose to do it with a partner. You will have some in each group, based on their multiple intelligences.

The higher thinkers in our classroom who are at the level of evaluating might be asked to evaluate a PowerPoint. They might want to do it individually, intrapersonal, or they might choose to do it with a partner, which would be interpersonal. Still, both groups are evaluating a PowerPoint.

Again, it is the same assignment, but the teacher offers students two different choices. We can basically pick any two multiple intelligences and create experiences for students from which they can choose.

It sounds so obvious, but very few teachers do it. To get a no failing students outcome, focus on your students who are struggling and create activities where they will be successful.

Free No Failing Students Resources...

I have gathered multiple intelligence activities for you to motivate your students. All of the following resources are free and downloadable...

- Elementary school multiple intelligence activities

- Middle school multiple intelligence activities

- High school multiple intelligence activities

To download your Free Productivity package (which includes these multiple intelligence activities), go to:

http://www.NoFailingStudents.com

Either click the link if you are using a digital book reader or type it into your browser.

STEP 5:

SCORE PRACTICE WORK ON COMPLETION

Score Practice Work on Completion

Step five is to score this practice work from the previous step on completion, rather than accuracy. The mistake many teachers make is to score practice work for accuracy, rather than completion.

The reason for this is that students are still in the process of learning the new material. You should give feedback early in the learning process, but save grading for later in the learning process. We want to evaluate after they have had time to practice and learn. Quizzes and tests still get graded for accuracy, but the practice assignments themselves should always be graded for completion.

Free No Failing Students Resources...

I have prepared a set of grading tools that can help you when assessing students. All of the following resources are free and downloadable...

- Grading Smarter Formula

- Grading Success Tips

To download your Free Productivity package (which includes the Grading Smarter Formula and Grading Success Tips), go to:

http://www.NoFailingStudents.com

Either click the link if you are using a digital book reader or type it into your browser.

STEP 6:

SCAFFOLD ASSESSMENTS

STEP 6:

Scaffold Assessments

Step six is to scaffold assessments for students who scored less than 65% on the last assessment. I want you to zero in here on the *last* assessment. So if the last assessment was more than 65%, they do not need to have their assessment scaffolded.

There are three very specific types of scaffolding that I recommend that don't water down the content, but do allow students to achieve success.

Scaffold 1: Fewer Choices

The first scaffold you can make is to "offer fewer choices." For example, you might have a definition and have three vocabulary words to choose from, rather than ten.

Instead of matching 10 words to 10 definitions, one of the ways to scaffold is to shorten the number of choices and have three definitions and three words so students have less to look at and fewer choices.

One way to do this is with a word bank. Instead of a fill-in-the-blank format with no suggestions for the students, provide a word bank of possible answers from which the students can choose. This scaffold doesn't change the content being taught, and it doesn't change the standard that you're teaching, but it allows students to be successful in a situation where they otherwise were not.

Scaffold 2: Chunking

A second scaffold you can make is called chunking. An example of chunking would be to take an assessment that matches 20 vocabulary terms to 20 definitions and break it up into sets of five. In other words, you'll have five vocabulary words and five definitions. Then, you go on to the next five vocabulary words and five definitions.

I love this scaffold because we aren't changing how much we expect the students to know. They still need to know all the vocabulary words. If there were 20 vocabulary words or 20 facts or 20 theorems that they are supposed to know, they still have to know all 20 of them. But when you get to the assessment, you're going to chunk off the information and block off five and then block off another five. Continue five at a time until they're all blocked.

Chunking doesn't water down the curriculum. It just makes the assessment an easier way for students to show you what they know. You're still evaluating the same standard at the same level and covering the same content, but you're eliminating things that trip up students and cause them to fail.

Scaffold 3: Graphic Organizer

The third scaffold you can make is to provide students with a graphic organizer to complete. For example, you might have vocabulary from four different units. Take a graphic organizer that has four parts to it, and separate the vocabulary from the four units into the four parts of the graphic organizer. This way, a student will be able to recall the vocabulary from that particular unit.

CHUNKED ELEMENTARY VOCABULARY
QUIZ EXAMPLE

(Include no more than 15 words)

Directions: Fill in the blanks below with the correct word below.

Enormous   Estimate   Effect
Diagram   Different   Drowsy

1._____
   calculate roughly or rough calculation

2._____
   huge, gigantic, giant

3._____
   result or accomplish

4._____
   sleepy, dozy

5._____
   unlike or separate

6._____
   drawing, sketch

Directions: Fill in the blanks below with the correct words below.

Amaze   Arranged   Analyze
Cooperation   Connection   Cycle

7._____

   round or a bike, pedal

8._____

   teamwork

9._____

   link, relationship

10._____

   order, organize

11._____

   examine, inspect

12._____

   surprise, shock

Date _____   Name _____

ELEMENTARY VOCABULARY
PRE-ASSESSMENT EXAMPLE
(Include no more than 15 words)

Directions: Fill in the blanks below with the correct word from the top of the page.

Amaze   Analyze   Arranged
Connection   Cooperation   Cycle
Diagram   Different   Drowsy
Effect   Enormous   Estimate

1._____

calculate roughly or rough calculation

2._____

huge, gigantic, giant

3._____

result or accomplish

4._____

sleepy, dozy

5._____

unlike or separate

6._____

drawing, sketch

7._____

round or a bike, pedal

8._____
teamwork

9._____
link, relationship

10._____
order, organize

11._____
examine, inspect

12._____
surprise, shock

Date _____ Name _____

FEWER CHOICES ELEMENTARY
VOCABULARY QUIZ EXAMPLE
(Include no more than 15 words)

Directions: Circle the word or words under each line that go with the words above the line.

1. calculate roughly or rough calculation
   Enormous   Estimate   Effect

2. huge, gigantic, giant
   Enormous   Estimate   Effect

3. result or accomplish
   Enormous   Estimate   Effect

4. sleepy, dozy
   Diagram   Different   Drowsy

5. unlike or separate
   Diagram   Different   Describe

6. drawing, sketch
   Diagram   Different   Drowsy

7. round or a bike, pedal
   Cooperation   Connection   Cycle

8. teamwork
   Cooperation   Connection   Cycle

9. link, relationship
   Cooperation   Connection   Cycle

10. <u>order, organize</u>
    Amaze   Arranged   Analyze

11. <u>examine, inspect</u>
    Amaze   Arranged   Analyze

12. <u>surprise, shock</u>
    Amaze   Arranged   Analyze

Date _____ Name _____

GRAPHIC ORGANIZER ELEMENTARY VOCABULARY QUIZ EXAMPLE

Directions: Use the words at the top to fill in the blanks correctly in each box.

Amaze	Arranged	Analyze
Cooperation	Connection	Cycle
Enormous	Estimate	Effect
Diagram	Different	Drowsy

1._____ order, organize	4._____ round, bike, pedal
2._____ examine, inspect	5._____ teamwork
3._____ surprise, shock	6._____ link, relationship
7._____ sleepy, dozy	10._____ calculate roughly or rough calculation
8._____ unlike or separate	11._____ huge, gigantic, giant
9._____ drawing, sketch	12._____ result or accomplish

CHUNKED MIDDLE SCHOOL
VOCABULARY QUIZ EXAMPLE
(Include no more than 30 words at a time)

Directions: Fill in the blanks below with the correct word listed below.

Abdicate	Abrasive	Abruptly
Belligerent	Bewilder	Bias

1._____
    hostile, aggressive, threatening

2. _____
    baffle, mystify, puzzle, confuse

3._____
    prejudice, partiality, favoritism

4._____
    corrosive, cutting, biting

5. _____
    suddenly, unexpectedly, curtly, bluntly

6._____
    resign, retire, step down

Directions: Fill in the blanks below with the correct word listed below.

Candor	Casualty	Cause
Dawdle	Deceitful	Demeanor

7._____

    dishonest, untruthful, false

8._____

    manner, air, attitude, appearance, look

9._____

    victim, fatality, loss, MIA

10. _____

    source, root, or principle, ideal

11._____

    frankness, openness, honesty

12._____

    linger, dally, idle

Directions: Fill in the blanks below with the correct word listed below.

Emphasize   **Estimate**   **Evaluate**
Impartial   **Inevitable**   **Irrelevant**

13._____approsimate, estimation

14._____stress, underline, highlight

15._____assess, judge, gauge

16._____immaterial, unconnected, unrelated

17._____unavoidable, inescapable, inexorable

18._____unbiased, unprejudiced, neutral

Directions: Fill in the blanks below with the correct word listed below.

Narrate   Necessity   Negligent
Persuasive   Prediction   Prominent

19._____essential, prerequisite, necessary

20._____tell, relate, recount, describe

21._____neglectful, careless, irresponsible

22._____important, notable, famous

23._____forecast, prophecy, prognosis

24._____convincing, compelling, forceful

Date _____ Name _____

FEWER CHOICES MIDDLE SCHOOL
VOCABULARY QUIZ EXAMPLE
(Include no more than 30 words at a time)

Directions: Circle the word or words under each line that go with the words above the line.

1. source, root, or principle, ideal
   Candor   Casualty   Cause

2. baffle, mystify, puzzle, confuse
   Belligerent   Bewilder   Bias

3. resign, retire, step down
   Abdicate   Abrasive   Abruptly

4. hostile, aggressive, threatening
   Belligerent   Bewilder   Bias

5. victim, fatality, loss, MIA
   Candor   Casualty   Cause

6. manner, air, attitude, appearance, look
   Dawdle   Deceitful   Demeanor

7. frankness, openness, honesty
   Candor   Casualty   Cause

8. dishonest, untruthful, false
   Dawdle   Deceitful   Demeanor

9. corrosive, cutting, biting
   Abdicate   Abrasive   Abruptly

10. <u>suddenly, unexpectedly, curtly, bluntly</u>
    Abdicate   Abrasive   Abruptly

11. <u>prejudice, partiality, favoritism</u>
    Belligerent   Bewilder   Bias

12. <u>linger, dally, idle</u>
    Dawdle   Deceitful   Demeanor

Directions: Circle the word under the line that goes with the words above the line.

13. <u>approximate, estimation</u>
    Emphasize   Estimate   Evaluate

14. <u>stress, underline, highlight</u>
    Emphasize   Estimate   Evaluate

15. <u>assess, judge, gauge</u>
    Emphasize   Estimate   Evaluate

16. <u>immaterial, unconnected, unrelated</u>
    Impartial   Inevitable   Irrelevant

17. <u>unavoidable, inescapable, inexorable</u>
    Impartial   Inevitable   Irrelevant

18. <u>unbiased, unprejudiced, neutral</u>
    Impartial   Inevitable   Irrelevant

19. <u>essential prerequisite, necessary</u>
    Narrate   Necessity   Negligent

20. <u>tell, relate, recount, describe</u>
    Narrate   Necessity   Negligent

21. <u>neglectful, careless, irresponsible</u>
    Narrate   Necessity   Negligent

22. <u>important, notable, famous</u>
    Persuasive   Prediction   Prominent

23. <u>forecast, prophecy, prognosis</u>
    Persuasive   Prediction   Prominent

24. <u>convincing, compelling, forceful</u>
    Persuasive   Prediction   Prominent

GRAPHIC ORGANIZER MIDDLE SCHOOL VOCABULARY QUIZ EXAMPLE

Directions: Use the words at the top of each box to fill in the blanks correctly in each box.

Abdicate	Abrasive	Abruptly
Belligerent	Bewilder	Bias
Candor	Casualty	Cause
Dawdle	Deceitful	Demeanor

1._____
   source, root, principle,
   ideal

2._____
   victim, fatality, loss, MIA

3._____
   frankness, openness,
   honesty

4._____
   baffle, mystify, puzzle,
   confuse

5._____
   hostile, aggressive,
   threatening

6._____
   prejudice, partiality,
   favoritism

7._____
   resign, retire, step down

8._____
   corrosive, cutting, biting

9._____
   suddenly, unexpectedly,
   curtly, bluntly

10._____
    manner, air, attitude,
    appearance, look

11._____
    dishonest, untruthful,
    false

12._____
    linger, dally, idle

Directions: Use the words at the top of each box to fill in the blanks correctly in each box.

Emphasize	Estimate	Evaluate
Impartial	Inevitable	Irrelevant
Narrate	Necessity	Negligent
Persuasive	Prediction	Prominent

13._____
    approximate, estimation
 	
14._____
    stress, underline,
    highlight
 	
15._____
    assess, judge, gauge
	16._____
	    immaterial,
	    unconnected, unrelated
	
	17._____
	    unavoidable,
	    inescapable, inexorable
	
	18._____
	    unbiased, unprejudiced,
	    neutral

19._____
    essential, prerequisite,
    necessary
 	
20._____
    tell, relate, recount,
    describe
 	
21._____
    neglectful, careless,
    irresponsible
	22._____
	    important, notable,
	    famous
	
	23._____
	    forecast, prophecy,
	    prognosis
	
	24._____
	    convincing, compelling,
	    forceful

Date _____   Name _____

HIGH SCHOOL VOCABULARY
PRE-ASSESSMENT EXAMPLE
(Include no more than 30 words at a time)

Directions: Fill in the blanks below with the correct word from the top of the page.

Aberration	Abstract	Accolade
Cajole	Callous	Capitulate
Dearth	Decadence	Deference
Effervescent	Egregious	Equivocal

1. _____
   conceptual, intellectual, extract, separate

2. _____
   anomaly, deviation, divergence, abnormality

3._____
   honor, privilege, award, gift, title

4._____
   surrender, yield, submit

5._____
   heartless, unfeeling, uncaring, cold

6._____
   persuade, coax, seduce

7._____
   dissipation, corruption, sin, immorality

8._____

respect, respectfulness, dutifulness

9._____

lack, scarcity, shortage, shortfall, want, deficiency

10._____

fizzy, sparkling, carbonated, gassy, bubbly

11._____

ambiguous, indefinite, noncommittal, vague

12._____

shocking, appalling, terrible, awful

Directions: Fill in the blanks below with the correct word from the top of the page.

Haphazard	Heretic	Hinderance
Incidental	Indoctrinate	Intangible
Ponderous	Prerequisite	Preclude
Scrutinize	Substantiate	Surmise

13. _____
    dissenter, nonconformist, freethinker

14. _____
    obstacle, obstruction, handicap

15. _____
    random, unplanned, disorganized

16. _____
    impalpable, untouchable, abstract

17. _____
    brainwash, persuade, convince

18. _____
    less important, secondary, subsidiary

19. _____
    clumsy, heavy, awkward, slow

20. _____
    precondition, essential, requirement

21. _____
    prevent, stop, bar, hinder

22. _____

    guess, suspect, conclude

23. _____

    examine, inspect, survey

24. _____

    prove, support, uphold

CHUNKED HIGH SCHOOL
VOCABULARY QUIZ EXAMPLE
(Include no more than 30 words at a time)

Directions: Fill in the blanks with the correct word listed below.

Aberration	Abstract	Accolade
Cajole	Callous	Capitulate

1. _____
   conceptual, intellectual, extract, separate

2. _____
   anomaly, deviation, divergence, abnormality

3. _____
   honor, privilege, award, gift, title

4. _____
   surrender, yield, submit

5. _____
   heartless, unfeeling, uncaring, cold

6. _____
   persuade, coax, seduce

Directions: Fill in the blanks below with the correct word listed below.

Dearth   Deference   Decadence
Equivocal   Effervescent   Egregious

7. _____
    dissipation, corruption, sin, immorality

8. _____
    respect, respectfulness, dutifulness

9. _____
    lack, scarcity, shortage, shortfall, want, deficiency

10._____
    fizzy, sparkling, carbonated, gassy, bubbly

11._____
    ambiguous, indefinite, noncommittal, vague

12._____
    shocking, appalling, terrible, awful

Directions: Fill in the blanks below with the correct word listed below.

Haphazard   Heretic   Hinderance
Incidental   Indoctrinate   Intangible

13. _____
    dissenter, nonconformist, freethinker

14. _____
    obstacle, obstruction, handicap

15. _____
    random, unplanned, disorganized

16. _____
    impalpable, untouchable, abstract

17. _____
    brainwash, persuade, convince

18. _____
    less important, secondary, subsidiary

Directions: Fill in the blanks below with the correct word listed below.

Ponderous	Preclude	Prerequisite
Scrutinize	Substantiate	Surmise

19. _____
   clumsy, heavy, awkward, slow

20. _____
   precondition, essential, requirement

21. _____
   prevent, stop, bar, hinder

22. _____
   guess, suspect, conclude

23. _____
   examine, inspect, survey

24. _____
   prove, support, uphold

FEWER CHOICES HIGH SCHOOL
VOCABULARY QUIZ EXAMPLE
(Include no more than 30 words at a time)

Directions: Circle the word or words under each line that go with the words above the line.

1. conceptual, intellectual, extract, separate
   Aberration   Abstract   Accolade

2. anomaly, deviation, divergence, abnormality
   Aberration   Abstract   Accolade

3. honor, privilege, award, gift, title
   Aberration   Abstract   Accolade

4. surrender, yield, submit
   Cajole   Callous   Capitulate

5. heartless, unfeeling, uncaring, cold
   Cajole   Callous   Capitulate

6. persuade, coax, seduce
   Cajole   Callous   Capitulate

7. dissipation, corruption, sin, immorality
   Dearth   Deference   Decadence

8. respect, respectfulness, dutifulness
   Dearth   Deference   Decadence

9. lack, scarcity, shortage, shortfall, want, deficiency_____

Dearth   Deference   Decadence

10. fizzy, sparkling, carbonated, gassy, bubbly

Equivocal   Effervescent   Egregious

11. ambiguous, indefinite, noncommittal, vague

Equivocal   Effervescent   Egregious

12. shocking, appalling, terrible, awful

Equivocal   Effervescent   Egregious

Directions: Circle the word under the line that goes with the words above the line.

13. dissenter, nonconformist, freethinker

Haphazard   Heretic   Hinderance

14. obstacle, obstruction, handicap

Haphazard   Heretic   Hinderance

15. random, unplanned, disorganized

Haphazard   Heretic   Hinderance

16. impalpable, untouchable, abstract

Incidental   Indoctrinate   Intangible

17. brainwash, persuade, convince

Incidental   Indoctrinate   Intangible

18. less important, secondary, subsidiary

Incidental   Indoctrinate   Intangible

19. <u>clumsy, heavy, awkward, slow</u>
    Ponderous   Preclude   Prerequisite

20. <u>precondition, essential, requirement</u>
    Ponderous   Preclude   Prerequisite

21. <u>prevent, stop, bar, hinder</u>
    Ponderous   Preclude   Prerequisite

22. <u>guess, suspect, conclude</u>
    Scrutinize   Substantiate   Surmise

23. <u>examine, inspect, survey</u>
    Scrutinize   Substantiate   Surmise

24. <u>prove, support, uphold</u>
    Scrutinize   Substantiate   Surmise

GRAPHIC ORGANIZER HIGH SCHOOL VOCABULARY QUIZ EXAMPLE

Directions: Use the words at the top of the page to fill in the blanks correctly in each box.

Aberration	Abstract	Accolade
Cajole	Callous	Capitulate
Dearth	Deference	Decadence
Equivocal	Effervescent	Egregious

1._____ conceptual, intellectual, extract, separate	4._____ persuade, coax, seduce 5._____ heartless, unfeeling, uncaring, cold
2._____ anomaly, deviation, divergence, abnormality	
3._____ honor, privilege, award, gift, title	6._____ surrender, yield, submit
7._____ dissipation corruption, sin, immorality	10._____ fizzy, sparkling, carbonated, gassy, bubbly
8._____ respect, respectfulness, dutifulness	11._____ ambiguous, indefinite, noncommittal vague
9._____ lack, scarcity, shortage, shortfall, want, deficiency	12._____ shocking, appalling, terrible, awful

Directions: Use the words at the top of the page to fill in the blanks correctly in each box.

Haphazard	Heretic	Hinderance
Incidental	Indoctrinate	Intangible
Ponderous	Prerequisite	Preclude
Scrutinize	Substantiate	Surmise

13._____
  dissenter, nonconformist,
  freethinker
	16._____
	  impalpable, untouchable,
	  abstract

14._____
  obstacle, obstruction,
  handicap
	17._____
	  brainwash, persuade,
	  convince

15._____
  random, unplanned,
  disorganized
	18._____
	  less important,
	  secondary, subsidiary

19._____
  clumsy, heavy, awkward,
  slow
 	
20._____
  precondition, essential,
  requirement
 	
21._____
  prevent, stop, bar, hinder
	22._____
	  guess, suspect, conclude
	
	23._____
	  examine, inspect, survey
	
	24._____
	  prove, support, uphold

Free No Failing Students Resources...

I have designed nine scaffold templates for you to use with your students for their success. All of the following resources are free and downloadable.

- Three elementary school scaffold templates

- Three middle school scaffold templates

- Three high school scaffold templates

To download your Free Productivity package (which includes these nine scaffold templates), go to:

http://www.NoFailingStudents.com

Either click the link if you are using a digital book reader or type it into your browser.

STEP 7:

MULTIPLE OPPORTUNITIES FOR ASSESSMENTS

STEP 7:

Multiple Opportunities for Assessments

Step seven is allowing students to take assessments multiple times, replacing lower assessment scores with more recent, higher scores.

If a student scores below a "C" on an assessment, I require them to retake the assessment.

Some people think that that's not fair because students should never get another opportunity to take the test. Using a real life example, let's say you took a driver's test. If you failed it the first time, do you think you should never get a driver's license?

I know teachers who do this, and they average the original score with the new score, punishing the student for doing poorly on the first test and not giving them a reward for doing well on the second test. This is not a good idea because the "average" score is not an accurate measure of how much the student knows. The most accurate data that you have to measure a student's knowledge is the most recent data available.

Conclusion

If you implement these seven steps, you should expect to see no failing students.

Let me tell you about a recent experience I've had. I had the privilege of teaching fourth-quarter science to the seventh grade. I should point out that science is not my major. When I started teaching these students, I quickly realized that some of them were failing. When I checked, I found they had been failing during the first, second, and third quarters. So we had some work to do. By the end of the year, though, there were no failing students because we had applied the seven steps.

After so many days and quarters of failing, that's almost a miracle. I found that students had given up and there were behavior problems, too, which often come with a lack of success.

How did those students respond? What was it about the seven steps that captured those students and transformed them from no motivation to motivation, from misbehavior to no misbehavior?

They found out they could be successful. They realized that they could actually pass an assessment.

I modified assignments to meet their needs, offered them choices, and gave them multiple opportunities to take assessments.

I challenge you to try it and see what kind of results you get. It would be nice if we could have no failing students. We can do it one classroom at a time.

APPENDIX A

Reading List

VOCABULARY, APPROACH TO PROMOTING, and GROWTH LOOK LIKE. "Why vocabulary instruction needs to be long-term and comprehensive." *Teaching and learning vocabulary: Bringing research to practice* (2005): 27.

Griggs, Richard A, Alexandra Bujak-Johnson, and Derrick L Proctor. "Using common core vocabulary in text selection and teaching the introductory course." *Teaching of Psychology* 31.4 (2004): 265-269.

Banajee, Meher, Cynthia Dicarlo, and SARINTHA BURAS STRICKLIN. "Core vocabulary determination for toddlers." *Augmentative and Alternative Communication* 19.2 (2003): 67-73.

Griggs, Richard A, and Montserrat C Mitchell. "In search of introductory psychology's classic core vocabulary." *Teaching of Psychology* (2002).

Hyland, Ken, and Polly Tse. "Is there an "academic vocabulary"?." *TESOL quarterly* 41.2 (2007): 235-253.

Lee, David YW. "Defining core vocabulary and tracking its distribution across spoken and written genres." *Journal of English linguistics* 29.3 (2001): 250-278.

Diaz-Rico, Lynne T, and Kathryn Z Weed. *The crosscultural, language, and academic development handbook: A complete K-12 reference guide.* Boston: Allyn and Bacon, 2002.

Stein, Gabriele. "Developing your English vocabulary." *A systematic new approach* (2002).

Beck, Isabel L, Margaret G McKeown, and Linda Kucan. *Bringing words to life: Robust vocabulary instruction.* Guilford Press, 2013.

Gunning, Thomas G. *Creating literacy instruction for all students.* Pearson Higher Ed, 2012.

Daniels, Harvey et al. "Subjects Matter: Every Teacher's Guide to Content-Are Reading." (2007).

Marzano, Robert J, and Julia A Simms. *Vocabulary for the common core.* Marzano Research Laboratory, 2013.

Multiple Intelligences Reading List Armstrong, Thomas. *Multiple intelligences in the classroom.* Ascd, 2009.

Silver, Harvey F, Richard W Strong, and Matthew J Perini. *So each may learn: Integrating learning styles and multiple intelligences.*. Association for Supervision and Curriculum Development, 1703 North Beauregard Street, Alexandria, VA 22311-1714, 2000.

Gardner, Howard. "Multiple intelligences after twenty years." *American Educational Research Association, Chicago, Illinois* 21 (2003).

Abraham, Sheela J. "Multiple Intelligences in the Classroom." *Masalah Pendidikan* 24 (2001): 1-14.Armstrong, T. (2010). Multiple intelligences.

Heming, Andrea Lauren. "Multiple intelligences in the classroom." (2008).

Krechevsky, Mara, and Steve Seidel. "Minds at work: Applying multiple intelligences in the classroom." *Understanding Learning: Influences and Outcomes* 2 (2001): 44.

Noble, Toni. "Integrating the revised Bloom's taxonomy with multiple intelligences: A planning tool for curriculum differentiation." *The Teachers College Record* 106.1 (2004): 193-211.

Chan, David W. "Adjustment problems and multiple intelligences among gifted students in Hong Kong: The development of the revised

Student Adjustment Problems Inventory." *High Ability Studies* 14.1 (2003): 41-54.

Furnham, Adrian. "Self-estimates of intelligence: Culture and gender difference in self and other estimates of both general (g) and multiple intelligences." *Personality and Individual Differences* 31.8 (2001): 1381-1405.

Waterhouse, Lynn. "Multiple intelligences, the Mozart effect, and emotional intelligence: A critical review." *Educational Psychologist* 41.4 (2006): 207-225.

Armstrong, Thomas. *In their own way: discovering and encouraging your child's multiple intelligences.* Penguin, 2000.

Anderson, Lorin W et al. "A taxonomy for learning, teaching, and assessing: A revision of Bloom's taxonomy of educational objectives, abridged edition." *White Plains, NY: Longman* (2001).

Buckley, Jim, and Christopher Exton. "Bloom's taxonomy: a framework for assessing programmers' knowledge of software systems." *Program Comprehension, 2003. 11th IEEE International Workshop on* 10 May. 2003: 165-174.

Atherton, James S. "Learning and teaching." *Bloom's taxonomy* (2011).

Marzano, Robert J. *Designing a New Taxonomy of Educational Objectives. Experts in Assessment.* Corwin Press, Inc., A Sage Publications Company, 2455 Teller Road, Thousand Oaks, CA 91320-2218 (paperback: ISBN-0-8039-6836-1, $27.95; library edition: ISBN-0-8039-6835-3, $61.95), 2001.

Krathwohl, David R. "A revision of Bloom's taxonomy: An overview." *Theory into practice* 41.4 (2002): 212-218.

Forehand, Mary. "Bloom's taxonomy." *Emerging perspectives on learning, teaching, and technology* (2010): 41-47.

Huitt, William. "Bloom et al.'s taxonomy of the cognitive domain." *Educational Psychology Interactive* 22 (2004).

Hopson, Michael H, Richard L Simms, and Gerald A Knezek. "Using a technology-enriched environment to improve higher-order thinking skills." *Journal of Research on Technology in Education* 34.2 (2001): 109-119.

Forster, Margaret. "Higher order thinking skills." *Research Developments* 11.11 (2004): 1.

Zohar, Anat, and Yehudit J Dori. "Higher order thinking skills and low-achieving students: Are they mutually exclusive?." *The Journal of the Learning Sciences* 12.2 (2003): 145-181.

Miri, Barak, Ben-Chaim David, and Zoller Uri. "Purposely teaching for the promotion of higher-order thinking skills: A case of critical thinking." *Research in science education* 37.4 (2007): 353-369.

McLoughlin, Catherine, and Mark JW Lee. "Social software and participatory learning: Pedagogical choices with technology affordances in the Web 2.0 era." *ICT: Providing choices for learners and learning. Proceedings ascilite Singapore 2007* Dec. 2007: 664-675.

Korpelainen, Eija, and Mari Kira. "Employees' choices in learning how to use information and communication technology systems at work: strategies and approaches." *International Journal of Training and Development* 14.1 (2010): 32-53.

Lizzio, Alf, and Keithia Wilson. "Enhancing the effectiveness of self-managed learning groups: understanding students' choices and concerns." *Studies in Higher Education* 31.6 (2006): 689-703.

Hill, Grant M, and Brian Cleven. "A comparison of students' choices of 9th grade physical education activities by ethnicity." *The high school journal* (2005): 16-23.

Hannover, Bettina, and Ursula Kessels. "Self-to-prototype matching as a strategy for making academic choices. Why high school students do not like math and science." *Learning and instruction* 14.1 (2004): 51-67.

Deasy, Richard J. *Critical Links: Learning in the Arts and Student Academic and Social Development.* Arts Education Partnership, One Massachusetts Ave., NW, Suite 700, Washington, DC 20001-1431. Web site: http://www. aep-arts. org/., 2002.

O'Neill, Geraldine, and Tim McMahon. "Student-centred learning: What does it mean for students and lecturers." *Emerging issues in the practice of university learning and teaching* 1 (2005).

Karns, Gary L. "An update of marketing student perceptions of learning activities: Structure, preferences, and effectiveness." *Journal of marketing education* 27.2 (2005): 163-171.

Sparrow, Len, Heather Sparrow, and Paul Swan. "Student centred learning: Is it possible." *Flexible futures in tertiary teaching. Proceedings of the 9th Annual Teaching Learning Forum* Feb. 2000: 2-4.

Dragga, Sam. "The effects of praiseworthy grading on students and teachers." *Journal of Teaching Writing* 7.1 (2010): 41-50.

Salend, Spencer J, and Laurel M Garrick Duhaney. "Grading students in inclusive settings." *Teaching Exceptional Children* 34.3 (2002): 8-15.

Nitko, Anthony J. *Educational assessment of students.* Prentice-Hall, Inc., PO Box 11071, Des Moines, IA 50336-1071, 2001.

Speck, Bruce W. *Grading Students' Classroom Writing: Issues and Strategies. ASHE-ERIC Higher Education Report, Volume 27, Number 3.* ERIC Clearinghouse on Higher Education, The George Washington University, One Dupont Circle, NW, Suite 630, Washington, DC 20036-1183, 2000.

Walvoord, Barbara E, and Virginia Johnson Anderson. *Effective grading: A tool for learning and assessment in college.* John Wiley & Sons, 2011.

Brookhart, Susan M. *Grading and learning: Practices that support student achievement.* Solution Tree Press, 2011.

Swinton, Omari H. "The effect of effort grading on learning." *Economics of Education Review* 29.6 (2010): 1176-1182.

Sadler, Philip M, and Eddie Good. "The impact of self-and peer-grading on student learning." *Educational assessment* 11.1 (2006): 1-31.

Ewell, Peter T. "Grading student learning: You have to start somewhere." *Measuring Up* (2002): 73-76.

Stevens, Dannelle D, and Antonia J Levi. *Introduction to rubrics: An assessment tool to save grading time, convey effective feedback, and promote student learning.* Stylus Publishing, LLC, 2011.

Shepard, Lorrie A. "The role of assessment in a learning culture." *Educational researcher* (2000): 4-14.

Shepard, Lorrie A. "Linking Formative Assessment to Scaffolding." *Educational leadership* 63.3 (2005): 66-70.

Siegel, Marcelle A. "Striving for equitable classroom assessments for linguistic minorities: Strategies for and effects of revising life science items." *Journal of Research in Science Teaching* 44.6 (2007): 864-881.

Guskey, Thomas R. "How classroom assessments improve learning." *Educational Leadership* 60.5 (2003): 6-11.

Andrade, Heidi, and Gregory J Cizek. *Handbook of formative assessment.* Heidi Andrade & Gregory J Cizek. Routledge, 2010.

Stiggins, Rick, and Rick DuFour. "Maximizing the power of formative assessments." *Phi Delta Kappan* 90.9 (2009): 640-644.

Shepard, Lome A. "Formative assessment: Caveat emptor." *The future of assessment: Shaping teaching and learning* (2008): 279-303.

Ainsworth, Larry, and Donald Viegut. *Common formative assessments: How to connect standards-based instruction and assessment.* Larry Ainsworth & Donald Viegut. SAGE, 2006.

Carless, David. "From testing to productive student learning: Implementing formative assessment in Confucian-heritage settings." *Journal of Second Language Teaching and Research. Volume* 1.2 (2011): 155-158.

Guskey, Thomas R. "How classroom assessments improve learning." *Educational Leadership* 60.5 (2003): 6-11.

Stiggins, Richard J. "Assessment crisis: The absence of assessment for learning." *Phi Delta Kappan* 83.10 (2002): 758-765.

Stiggins, Richard J. *Student-involved assessment for learning.* Prentice Hall, 2005.

O'Connor, Ken. *How to grade for learning: Linking grades to standards.* SkyLight Professional

Development, 2626 South Clearbrook Drive, Arlington Heights, IL 60005, 2002.

O'Connor, Ken. *A repair kit for grading: 15 fixes for broken grades*. Pearson, 2011.

Carr, Judy F, and Douglas E Harris. *Succeeding with standards: Linking curriculum, assessment, and action planning*. ASCD, 2001.

Sandmann, Alexa L, and John F Ahern. *Linking Literature with Life: The NCSS Standards and Children's Literature for the Middle Grades. NCSS Bulletin.* National Council for the Social Studies, 8555 Sixteenth Street, Suite 500, Silver Spring, MD 20910, 2002.

Broh, Beckett A. "Linking extracurricular programming to academic achievement: Who benefits and why?." *Sociology of Education* (2002): 69-95.

Mathis, William J. "The "Common Core" standards initiative: An effective reform tool." *Boulder and Tempe: Education and the Public Interest Center & Education Policy Research Unit. Retrieved July 29* (2010): 2010.

Carmichael, Sheila Byrd et al. "The State of State Standards--and the Common Core--in 2010." *Thomas B. Fordham Institute* (2010).

Miller, M David, Robert L Linn, and Norman E Gronlund. *Measurement and assessment in teaching*. Pearson Higher Ed, 2012.

Beane, James, and Richard Lipka. "Guess Again: Will Changing the Grades Save Middle-Level Education?." *Educational Leadership* 63.7 (2006): 26.

Gears, Changing. "Classroom assessment: Minute by minute, day by day." *Assessment* 63.3 (2005).

APPENDIX B

ACTIONS AND PRODUCTS

Bloom's Taxonomy	Actions	Products
Creating	Designing Constructing Planning Producing Inventing Devising Making Animating Videocasting Storytelling Video editing Podcasting Collaborating Audio recording/editing Publishing Filming Programming Directing	Film Story Project Plan Painting New Game Song Media Product Advertisement Poem Cartoon Recipe News Article Magazine Multimedia presentation Play Rap Book/CD/DVD cover
Evaluating	Arguing Checking Hypothesizing Critiquing Experimenting Judging Testing Detecting Monitoring Networking Posting	Debate Panel Report Evaluation Speech Investigation Verdict Conclusion Persuasive Critique Court trial

	Conferencing Moderating Blogging Reviewing Simulating	News item Self-evaluation Summary Recommendation Conclusion
Analyzing	Comparing Organizing Deconstructing Attributing Outlining Structuring Integrating Separating Surveying Mashing Linking	Survey Database Mobile Abstract Report Graph Spreadsheet Checklist Chart Outline Questionnaire

ADDITIONAL COMMON CORE CRITICAL VOCABULARY QUIZZES

Date_____Name _____

Grade 3 Critical Verbs Quiz 1

Directions: Fill in the blanks with the correct word from the top of the page.

compare   contrast
describe   distinguish
identify   retell
demonstrate   draw
determine

1._____
                report, outline

2._____
                differentiate

3._____
              difference, variation

4._____
           spot, recognize, link, connect

5._____
             differentiate, tell apart

6._____
              say in your own words

7._____
            show, display, protest, march

8._____
              make a picture, tie

9._____

control, decide, discover

Date_____ Name _____

Grade 3 Critical Verbs Quiz 1 KEY

Directions: Fill in the blanks with the correct word from the top of the page.

compare	describe	draw
contrast	determine	identify
demonstrate	distinguish	retell

1._____describe_____report, outline

2._____compare_____differentiate

3._____contrast_____difference, variation

4._____identify_____spot, recognize, link, connect

5._____distinquish_____differentiate, tell apart

6._____retell_____say in your own words

7._____demonstrate_____show, display, protest, march

8._____draw_____make a picture, tie

9._____determine_____control, decide, discover

Date_____ Name_____

Grade 3 Critical Vocabulary Quiz 3

Directions: Fill in the blanks with the correct word from the top of each set of blanks.

connections   details
alliteration   central idea

1. _____parts, units

2. _____links, relationships

3. _____same letter or sound at the beginning

4. _____opinion, view, belief, feeling

illustrations   point of view
stanza   theme

5. _____pictures, drawings, sketches

6. _____main point

7. _____subject, topic, message

8. _____verse

Directions: Fill in the blanks with the correct word from the top of each set of blanks.

classify   explicitly
recognize   recount

9._____
order, organize, sort

10. _____
know, spot

11._____
retell, relate, report

12._____
precisely, clearly

Date_____ Name_____

Grade 3 Critical Vocabulary Quiz 3 KEY

1._____details_____parts, units

2._____connections_____links, relationships

3._____alliteration_____same letter or sound at the beginning

4._____point of view _____ opinion, view, belief, feeling

5._____illustrations_____pictures, drawings, sketches

6._____central idea _____ main point

7._____theme_____subject, topic, message

8._____stanza_____verse

9. _____classify _____ order, organize, sort

10._____ recognize _____ know, spot

11. _____ recount _____ retell, relate, report

12. _____ explicitly _____precisely, clearly

Date_____ Name _____

Grade 4 Critical Verbs Quiz 2

Directions: Fill in the blanks with the correct word from above each set of blanks.

suggest   comprehend   develop

1._____
recommend, propose

2._____
grow, start, begin

3._____
understand, include

support   organize
infer   refer

4._____
carry, help

5._____
mention

6._____
arrange, group, classify

7._____
conclude, interpret

integrate   paraphrase
summarize   interpret

8._____
reword, rewrite

9._____
combine, unite, mix

10._____
explain, understand, clarity

11._____
condense, outline

Date_____ Name _____

Grade 4 Critical Verbs Quiz 2 KEY

Directions: Fill in the blanks with the correct word from the top of the page.

comprehend   interpret   suggest
develop   organize   support
infer   paraphrase   refer
summarize   integrate

1. _____suggest_____recommend, propose

2. _____develop_____grow, start, begin

3. _____comprehend_____understand, include

4._____support_____carry, help

5. _____refer_____mention

6._____organize_____arrange, group, classify

7. _____infer_____conclude, interpret

8. _____paraphrase_____reword, rewrite

9. _____integrate_____combine, unite, mix

10.____interpret_____explain, understand, clarity

11._____summarize_____condense, outline

Date_____ Name _____

Grade 4 Critical Vocabulary Quiz 3

Directions: Fill in the blanks with the correct words listed below.

alliteration	connections	point of view
central idea	details	recognize
classify	illustrations	theme

1._____
parts, units

2._____
links, relationships

3._____
same letter of sound at the beginning

4._____
opinion, view, belief, feeling

5._____
pictures, drawings, sketches

6._____
main point

7._____
subject, topic, message

8. _____

order, organize, sort

9. _____

know, spot

Date_____Name _____

Grade 4 Critical Vocabulary Quiz 3 KEY

1. _____details_____parts, units

2. _____connections_____links, relationships

3. _____alliteration_____same letter of sound at the beginning

4. _____point of view_____ opinion, view, belief, feeling

5. ___illustrations___pictures, drawings, sketches

6. _____central idea_____ main point

7. _____theme_____subject, topic, message

8. _____ classify_____ order, organize, sort

9. _____ recognize _____ know, spot

Date_____   Name _____

Grade 5 Critical Verbs Quiz 1

Directions: Fill in the blanks with the correct verb listed below.

compare	determine	draw
locate	contrast	describe
explain	retell	demonstrate
distinguish	identify	

1._____report, outline

2. _____differentiate

3. _____difference, variation

4. _____spot, recognize, link, connect

5. _____differentiate, tell apart

6. _____say in your own words

7. _____show, display, protest, march

8. _____make a picture, tie

9. _____control, decide, discover

10._____find, discover, pinpoint

11._____describe

Date_____Name _____

Grade 5 Critical Verbs Quiz 1 KEY

Directions: Fill in the blanks with the correct word from the top of the page.

compare   determine   draw
locate   contrast   describe
explain   retell   demonstrate
distinguish   identify

1. _____describe_____report, outline

2. _____compare_____differentiate

3. _____contrast_____difference, variation

4. ____identify_____spot, recognize, link, connect

5. _____distinquish_____differentiate, tell apart

6. _____retell_____say in your own words

7. ___demonstrate__show, display, protest, march

8. _____draw_____make a picture, tie

9. _____determine_____control, decide, discover

10._____locate_____find, discover, pinpoint

11._____explain_____describe

Date_____   Name _____

Grade 5 Critical Nouns Quiz 1

Directions: Circle the word or words under each line that go with the words above the line.

1. <u>parts, units</u>
   connections   details   alliteration

2. <u>links, relationships</u>
   connections   details   alliteration

3. <u>same letter or sound at the beginning</u>
   details   alliteration   point of view

4. <u>opinion, view, belief, feeling</u>
   Details   alliteration   point of view

5. <u>pictures, drawings, sketches</u>
   Illustrations   central idea   stanza

6. <u>point</u>
   Illustrations   central idea   stanza

7. <u>subject, topic, message</u>
   point of view   stanza   theme

Date_____Name _____

Grade 5 Critical Nouns Quiz 1 KEY

Directions: Fill in the blanks with the correct words from the top of the page.

alliteration	details	point of view
central idea	illustrations	theme
connections		

1. _____details_____parts, units

2. _____connections_____links, relationships

3. _____alliteration____same letter or sound at the beginning

4. ____point of view__opinion, view, belief, feeling

5. ____illustrations___pictures, drawings, sketches

6. _____central idea_____main point

7. _____theme_____subject, topic, message

Date_____ Name _____

Middle School Critical Verbs Quiz 2

Directions: Use the words at the top of the page to fill in the blanks correctly in each box.

organize   refer   infer
integrate   interpret   paraphrase
summarize   analyze   articulate
cite   delineate   evaluate
trace   synthesize

1._____
        mention

2._____
        arrange, group, classify

3._____
        conclude, interpret

4._____
        reword, rewrite

5._____
        combine, unite, mix

6._____
        explain, understand, clarity

7._____
        quote, reproduce, summon

8._____
        examine, inspect, study

9._____

     fluent, expressive, communicate

10._____

     condense, outline

11._____

     find, outline, sign

12._____

     incorporate, integrate, blend

13._____

     assess, judge, rate

14._____

     describe, outline

Date_____ Name _____

Middle School Critical Verbs Quiz 2 KEY

Directions: Fill in the blanks with the correct word from the top of the page.

analyze   delineate   integrate
paraphrase   synthesize   articulate
evaluate   interpret   refer
trace   cite   infer
organize   summarize

1._____refer_____mention

2._____organize_____arrange, group, classify

3._____infer_____conclude, interpret

4._____paraphrase_____reword, rewrite

5._____integrate_____combine, unite, mix

6._____interpret_____explain, understand, clarity

7._____cite_____quote, reproduce, summon

8._____analyze_____examine, inspect, study

9._____articulate_____fluent, expressive, communicate

10._____summarize_____condense, outline

11._____trace_____find, outline, sign

12._____synthesize_____combine

13._____evaluate_____assess, judge, rate

14._____delineate_____describe, outline

Date_____   Name _____

High School Critical Nouns Quiz 2

Directions: Fill in the blanks with the correct critical noun.

1._____
construction, form

2._____
symbolic words

3._____
comparison

4._____
image, symbol

5._____
exchange

6._____
reasoning, explanation

7._____
word associations

8._____
state of mind

9._____

sound, voice

10._____

similarity

11._____

oratory, way with words

Date_____   Name_____

High School Critical
Vocabulary Quiz KEY

Directions: Fill in the blanks with the correct words from the top of the page.

analogy   figurative language
metaphor   simile
argument   interaction
mood   structure
connotative language   rhetoric
tone

1._____structure_____construction, form

2. _____figurative language _____symbolic words

3. _____simile_____comparison

4. _____metaphor_____image, symbol

5. _____interaction_____exchange

6. _____argument_____reasoning, explanation

7. ____connotive language____word associations

8. _____mood_____state of mind

9. _____tone_____sound, voice

10._____analogy_____ similarity

11._____rhetoric_____oratory, way with words

No Failing Students Bonus

Download the "No Failing Students Bonus" Productivity Package, which includes:

- Three pre-assessment templates
- Seven multiple intelligence surveys
- Ten analyzing activities
- Ten motivating multiple intelligence activities
- The grading smarter formula and grading success tips
- Nine scaffold assessment templates
- Newsletters
- And much more

To download your Free Productivity Package, click the link below (if you are using a digital reader) or type this URL into your browser…

http://www.NoFailingStudents.com

About the Author

Diane Hunt has a passion for helping teachers and schools to have No Failing Students. A teacher for over 25 years, Diane believes in a challenging, empowering, equitable curriculum. She uses active learning, multiple learning approaches, and varied assessments to have No Failing Students. Mrs. Hunt can show you how to motivate students, individualize instruction, ask higher-order questions, and utilize critical thinking skills. She also demonstrates how to grade without averaging, while using formative and summative assessments to maintain No Failing Students. Diane has presented at Common Core Saturdays, the Annual Michigan Charter School Conference, the National Conference on College and Career Readiness, and National High School Association Conferences.

Learn more about Diane Hunt by visiting www.NoFailingStudents.com.

CPSIA information can be obtained
at www.ICGtesting.com
Printed in the USA
LVHW04s1129190718
584314LV00026B/883/P